MIGO & ALI
LOVE FOR THE PROPHETS

By Zanib Mian
Illustrated by Tugrul Karacan

For Abdullah Mian, Abdurrahman Mian, Adam Zakariyah Goncalves, Elias Mikael Goncalves, Sara Alaa Mian, Mohammed Bilal Raie, Raees Raie, Aayan Raie, Zakariya Raie, Mugheesa Ahmed, Yusuf Ahmed, Zarah Ahmed, Ali Ahmed, Zain Piracha, Hassan Akhtar, Faisal Akhtar, Zaynah Sadiq, Ibrahim Sadiq, Zakariya Sadiq, Aasiyah Dossa, Muhammad Kumail Dossa, Leenah Yahya Currie, Aadam Asghar, Sulaymaan Farooq, Qasim Ali Hussain.

Published by Muslim Children's Books Ltd
Suite H, 31-33 College Road, Harrow, Middlesex HA1 1EJ

Muslim Children's Books

muslimchildrensbooks.co.uk

Published by Muslim Children's Books 2016
Text copyright © Zanib Mian, 2016
Illustrations copyright © Tugrul Karacan, 2016
Moral rights asserted.

ISBN 978-0-9955406-0-6

British Library Cataloguing in Publication Data. A catalogue record for this book is available from the British Library.

CONTENTS

Introduction

This book has been lovingly compiled, by popular demand from parents and children, after the author shared her love for the Prophets series on social media.

There are no depictions of any of the prophets or sahaba in this book. The content was written with reference to the Stories of the Prophets by Al Imam Ibn Kathir and has been reviewed for accuracy by Dr M.F Elshayyal PhD.

Scholarly reviews:

'This book is clearly the result of much hard work and painstaking effort. The stories are narrated in an age-appropriate, attractive dialogue format which bring up searching and meaningful questions for both the children and adults to ponder over. The book is vividly illustrated with a gentle sense of humour running through the stories, the main characters (MiGo & Ali) introduce special concepts then entice the reader into taking ownership of their learning and discovering more.' - *Dr Mohammad Fareed Elshayyal*

'I read the book and found it very beneficial for Muslim children, It is easy to read and understand. May Allah reward those behind it the greateast of rewards.' - *Sheikh Shady AlSuleiman*

Abbreviations and their meanings:

saw - stands for Sal Allahu Alayhi Wasalam/ May Allah's peace and blessings be upon him.

as - Stands for alayhi salaam, or alaihim salaam/ Upon him (or them) be peace.

ra - stands for Radi Allah An / May Allah be pleased with him or her.

ADAM

ALAYHI SALAM

Adam (as) was the first man

and the first prophet.

Allah made his human shape from sticky clay, just like you make things from play dough. Allah used lots of different colours to make Adam (as), and because all humans are children of Adam (as), we see people all over the world of different colours!

But then Allah did something that you and I can't do with play dough, and that nobody but Allah can do!

He breathed Life into Adam (as).

ALL the angels thought Adam was amazing, but another creature called Iblis did not, and he was very jealous of him.

8

Allah taught Adam (as) the names of things, like *bird, star, tree* and *cloud,* just like your parents taught you. Allah taught Adam to absolutely **Love** to learn about everything. That's why we all love to learn. When Adam (as) started to feel lonely,

ALLah made him a wife caLLed Hawwa (Eve).

Adam and Hawwa lived in a place called **Paradise,** which is more wonderful than we can imagine! Allah had only asked them NEVER to go near one particular tree. But after many years, Satan made them forget, and they ate fruit from that tree. Satan had tricked them and pretended to be their friend. Adam and Hawwa were very **sad** about what they did,

so ALLah forgave them.

He sent them to live on EARTH so Adam (as) could be His first messenger.

Question Time

Ali: Are Iblis and Shaytan the same, Migo?

Migo: Yes, those are both names for the devil. He can be called Iblis, Shaytan, or Satan in English.

Ali: What does it mean, that all of us are children of Adam (as)?

Migo: It means that he was the first man, then he had children, then his children had children, then his children's children had children...and that kept happening even until you were born!

Ali: Woah! So he's like my great granddad?

Migo: More like your great, great, great times a zillion granddad.

Ali: Haha.

Migo: Why do you think you love to learn and ask questions?

Ali: Because Adam (as) loved to learn, because Allah made him like that!

Migo: Absoluetly...now give me a kiss!

NUH
(Noah)
ALAYHI SALAM

Nuh (as), was a clever man. He used to tell all the people about Allah. He told them that there is only ONE God. But they didn't listen to him.

They thought statues and pictures, that humans had made with their own hands were God. Nuh (as) **tried** and **tried,** for many, many years to make them believe, but only some of them believed him, about Allah.

One day, ALLah toLd Nuh to make a big boat.

He told him how to make it. Nuh (as) worked hard all day and all night to build it and the angels helped him! The people made fun of him and thought he was SILLY, because there was no water nearby. But Allah had told Nuh that so much water was going to come, that all the houses and roads would be covered, like a sea, and that's why they would need the big boat.

Allah told Nuh (as) to take the **good** people and take two of each animal, bird and insect, on the boat where they would be safe.

Then the water came and there was so much that even the mountains were covered.

But Nuh (as), the **good** people and the animals and birds and insects, were safe. And when the water went away again, they thanked Allah and lived *happily.*

Question Time

Ali: Why did Nuh (as) make a boat, if there was no water and everyone was laughing at him?

Migo: Because Allah told him that water was coming. So much water, that everything would be covered. Allah wanted him to be ready to stay safe.

Ali: And keep the animals safe too!

Migo: Yes, and the animals. They went on the boat too.

Ali: But how did the water come? Did it rain?

Migo: Yes, it rained a lot! More rain than you've ever seen in your life. And water came from the cracks in the Earth.

Ali: I'm glad they all made it!

Migo: Me too, my bottle of juice, me too!

SALIH

ALAYHI SALAM

The prophet Salih (as), was sent by Allah to the people of Thamud. He told the people that Allah is one, and the lots of different gods they were praying to, were absolutely not real.

"We used to like you very much, but now you're telling us not to pray to our gods. Our dads used to pray to these gods, so we have to, too. We can't believe you about Allah." they said.

Then they told Salih, that he has to show them that he is Allah's messenger, by making a camel come from the mountains. They said it should be a girl camel, like they've never, ever seen before.

ALLah made that happen for Salih (as).

An amazing camel appeared!

The people couldn't believe their eyes. It was amazing! What's more,

the camel was a very special camel.

We all know that milk comes from cows, but milk also comes from camels. This camel was very special because it gave so much milk, that thousands of people could drink it. It also drank a lot of water.

Many of the people believed Salih (as) about Allah being the one and only God,

but some people didn't. Those people hated the special camel sent by Allah and they wanted to kill it.

One day, they managed to kill the poor camel.

Salih (as) wasn't happy at all. Hurting animals is bad, and this was a very special camel.

He told those people that they should feel sorry for what they have done, but they didn't feel sorry at all. In fact, they were even ruder. Salih (as) went to live in another place with the people that had been nice.

He didn't fight with the people who had killed the camel.

He went far away from them.

Then a big earthquake came where the people of Thamud lived.

Question Time

Ali: Migo, how can a camel come out of nowhere?

Migo: Allah can do anything He wants, my strawberry dumpling. He makes miracles happen, so that people believe what the messenger is telling them.

Ali: Then even when the camel came, some people didn't believe did they?

Migo: No. And they hurt that camel in the end, and they got punished for that.

Ali: Does Allah get sad if you hurt animals? Or only special ones like that camel?

Migo: Allah does not like it if we hurt any creature. We've got to be kind to animals. Haha, you have to be kind to me, Ali. Be a good boy and bring me a pecan and honey pie.

Ali: Haha, Migo, you're always hungry.

IBRAHIM

(Abraham)

ALAYHI SALAM

Ibrahim (as), was born at a time when some people thought the *stars*, planets, sun and **moon** were God; some thought that statues that they made from wood and stones was God; and some people even thought that kings were God!

Ibrahim (as) was very special, because ALLah had made him the **most** clever Little boy.

Even when he was a very little boy, he found it very funny that people could pray to things that they had made with their own hands. Things like we might make now with blocks or clay.

Even when he GREW UP, he thought it was not right, because he thought to himself that

if something can't get back up when you knock it down, it can't be God!

One night, Ibrahim (as) went to a cave, in a mountain to sit and think. He knew for sure that God *isn't made* from stones or wood. He saw a *star* in the dark night sky, and said to the people that it must be God. But then the star went away and so he said it couldn't be. Then he saw the **moon** and he said it must be God. But then the **moon** went away and so he said it couldn't be. Then he saw the sun and he said this one is greater, so it might be God. But then the sun went away and so he said it couldn't be!

Ibrahim (as) told the people what all this means.

The stars, moon, planets and sun are not Allah,

they are made by Allah

and come in front of our eyes and disappear again,

because Allah makes them do that.

Allah does not *disappear,*
he is there forever and he is always there...

The people who worshipped the planets and *stars* were very angry. Even his father was angry, because he used to make the statues that they prayed to, with his own hands. But Ibrahim (as) prayed to Allah to forgive him and tried to talk to the people. He was very strong in believing that nothing could happen to him unless Allah wanted it, so he wasn't scared of anybody or anything.

Ibrahim (as) tried to make everyone see

that these statues cannot be God,

because they cannot do anything for the people.

They can't even see!

But they just wouldn't listen. So one day, he went to the temple where their gods were, with an axe, and he smashed all of them,

except for the biggest one,

whose neck he hung his axe on.

When the people found the broken statues, they were absolutely furious! They guessed it must have been Ibrahim (as), so they went to ask him. Ibrahim (as) told them to ask their gods, because he knew that everyone knows they can't even speak.

THEN HE TOLD THEM IT MUST HAVE BEEN THE BIGGEST STATUE THAT SMASHED ALL THE SMALLER ONES.

He knew that the people would realise the biggest statue can't do that, and if he can't, he can't really be a god.

So the people decided to throw Ibrahim (as) into a fire.

They made a very very huge, enormous, raging fire. They tied up Ibrahim (as) - ready to throw him in.

The angel Gabriel (as) came to him and asked if he needed anything.

Ibrahim (as) was not scared, because he trusted Allah, so he said he didn't need anything from Gabriel. Then they threw Ibrahim (as) into the fire.

Allah has **POWER** over all things. He can even make **fire** cool, and that's what he did for Ibrahim (as). He told the **fire** to be cool and safe for him. So Ibrahim (as) sat in the **fire**, just as if it were a nice garden.

He thanked ALLah and feLt a Lot of Love for ALLah.

He didn't even feel scared or worried. He just felt love. The people who had tried to burn him had been standing around the fire and could feel how **HOT** it was, because it was only cool for Ibrahim (as). So when they saw him

come out of the fire compLeteLy fine,

as if he had walked out of a garden, they were *astonished!* They absolutely could not believe their eyes!

After that, many people secretly believed Ibrahim (as), but the king, Namrud, was FURIOUS, because he wanted people to believe that *he* was God! Ibrahim (as) became *very* famous, but still most people were angry and didn't believe him. His **wife** believed him and one man believed him.

His name was Lut (as) and he became a prophet.

They all left and went to travel to different lands.

Ibrahim (as) had a baby called Ismail (as), who also became a prophet.

One day Ibrahim (as) asked Allah to show him how he can bring a dead thing back to life. So Allah showed him, by making four dead birds come to life and FLY to him!

He spent his days

worshipping ALLah.

Question Time

Migo: Why did Ibrahim (as) decide that the moon and stars and sun can't be Allah?

Ali: I know! Because they come and go, they aren't always there. They are just something that Allah made. Like he made you and me. I'm glad he made you Migo.

Migo: Haha, I'm glad he made you too. But sometimes I wish he made you less jumpy!

Ali: Haha!

Migo: How did Ibrahim (as) prove to the people that the idols can't be God?

Ali: He took an axe and he smashed them to bits! Then he said it must have been the big one who smashed the little ones, which is so silly because even the big one can't move – so he can't be God.

Migo: Well done my bucket of berry juice!

Ali: But I can't believe that he went in the fire and it didn't burn him, Migo. How can that be?

Migo: Because fire is made by Allah, and Allah can control what it does. If He wants to make it cool instead of hot and burning, He can do that easily.

Ali: Ok!

ISMAIL

(Ishmael)

ALAYHI SALAM

One day, Allah told Prophet Ibrahim (as), to leave his wife, Hajar (as), and little baby son, Ismail (as), in a valley where nobody lived and where there was no fruit, no water and no trees. She asked him if Allah had said to leave them there, and he said yes. That made Hajar strong, because she knew very well, that if Allah had asked for it, He would look after them. Ibrahim (as) made dua for them before he left.

After the little bit of water that they had with them had finished, baby Ismail started to cry,

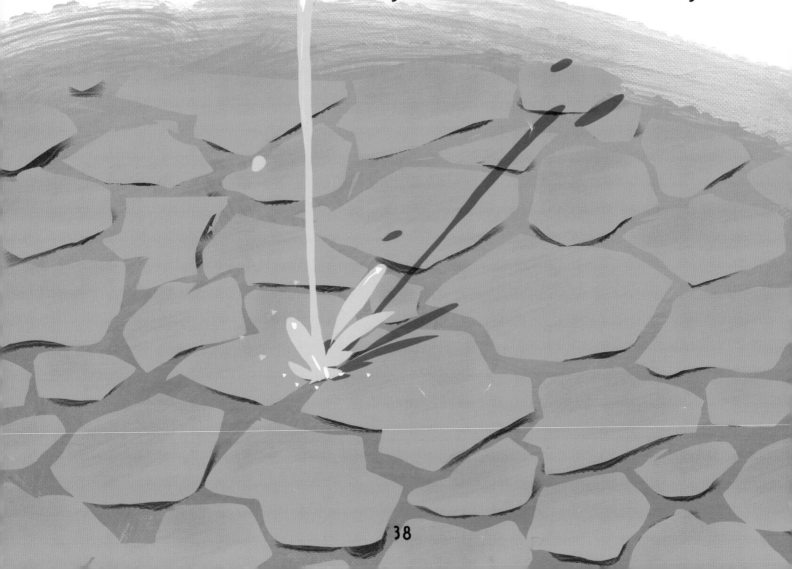

because he was *thirsty*. His mother tried and tried to look for water, but couldn't find any. There was a **mountain** called As-safa. She climbed it to see if she could see any people to help her. There was nobody, so she came down and ran to another **mountain** called Al-Marwa and climbed it to see if she could see people from there. She did that seven times.

That's why we do that during Hajj and Umrah.

When Hajar got to Al-Marwa for the last time, she heard a voice. So with hope, she asked who it is and if they could help. Then she saw! **Near baby Ismail there was an angel!** The angel kicked the earth and a spring of water came flowing out. **This water is very special and it is called Zamzam.** The well of Zamzam is still there after all these years, with lots of yummy water for us to drink, when we go for Hajj and Umrah. Hajar (as) happily gave the baby some water and drank some herself.

The angel told Hajar not to worry, and he told her that this is the house of Allah, which Ismail and his father will build - the Kaaba. Because there was now water there, slowly more people came to the valley and made their homes there too. When Ismail (as) had grown into a man, his father told him that

ALLAH HAS ORDERED HIM

TO BUILD A HOUSE

WITH ISMAIL'S HELP.

Ismail was pleased to help him do this great and wonderful job. He brought the heavy stones from all around, while his father built the house. When the walls of the house became high, Ismail brought a stone for his father to stand on and carry on building. While they were building, they kept praying to Allah to accept their work. Once the Kaaba was built, many people came for Hajj, to the house of Allah.

This house is full of blessings and it is a guidance. That's why Allah has said that all men and women must go for Hajj at least once in their lives. So once a year, in the month of Dhul Hijjah, believers go for Hajj.

People from all over the world go.

It is a beautiful journey indeed.

When you go In sha'Allah, you will see the Kaaba, and the mountains that Hajar climbed and you'll drink the special Zamzam water. You can even see the place where Ibrahim (as) stood on a stone, to build the Kaaba.

Question Time

Migo: During Umrah, why do we go from Safa to Marwah, and how many times do we do it?

Ali: Because that's what Hajar (as) did when she was looking for water. Seven times! It's quite hard you know Migo, I've done it.

Migo: And how did she finally find water?

Ali: Angel Jibreel (as) kicked the ground and Zamzam came out! I love Zamzam!

Migo: Right, my jelly baby, and who built the kaaba?

Ali: Ibrahim and Ismail (as)!

Migo: Great, you did some good listening!

ISHAAQ

ALAYHI SALAM

One day, when Ibrahim (as) was sitting thinking about all the things Allah had given him, three angels came to him. Ibrahim (as) didn't know they were angels. He asked them to come into his house and be his guests and have some food. But angels don't eat! So when they didn't eat, Ibrahim (as) started getting worried. He thought they might be people who want to hurt him. Then the angels told him not to worry.

They told him they were angels,

who had come to tell him and his wife

that they will be having a baby - Ishaaq (as).

Ibrahim (as) and his wife were shocked because they were now both very old, and old people do not usually have babies. But Allah can do anything and give any blessing to whoever he wants!

When Ishaaq (as) grew up, he had a son of his own, called Yaqub (Jacob). Yaqub (as) also became a prophet, and we will hear about him in the story of Yusuf (as).

Question Time

Ali: Migo, why don't angels eat?

Migo: Because, my butternut squash, they are different to humans. They don't need food or drink, and they don't burp or go to the toilet.

Ali: When do they sleep?

Migo: They don't sleep either. They just glorify Allah all day and all night.

Ali: Wow! What are they made of?

Migo: Angels are made of light, Ali.

Ali: Awesome!

YUSUF

(Joseph)

&

YAQUB

(Jacob)

ALAYHIMA SALAM

Yusuf (as) was Yaqub's (as) son. He had eleven broth

Yusuf (as) was very handsome and **strong** and he had

good manners. So did his brother, Binyamin/Benjamin (as).

Because they were such good boys, their father loved them.

Perhaps he loved them a teeny weeny bit more than the

other brothers.

THE OTHER BROTHERS WERE ALL VERY JEALOUS INDEED.

One day, Yusuf (as) ran to his father to tell him about a dream

he had. He said, 'Oh father! In my dream, eleven stars, the

sun and the **moon** were bowing down to me!'

His father was very **happy** to hear this, because he knew it

must mean that

Yusuf (as) would become a prophet, just like he was and his father was.

But he told him not to tell his brothers, because they would

be very, very jealous.

w, even though the brothers didn't know about the special *dream*, they were still very jealous and were making plans to kill Yusuf (as)!

One of the brothers said, "Let's just throw him in the well instead, then somebody will take him away."

They were silly enough to think that they could do something so bad, then become good, and it would all be ok.

So the brothers asked their father if he would allow Yusuf (as) to go out with them to have fun and play. Their father said he didn't want Yusuf (as) to go because he was afraid a WOlf might get him, if they don't take care of him. But they *begged* him to let him go and said that they were strong, so nothing could happen to Yusuf (as) while he is with them.

Finally their father agreed and off they all went.

Yusuf (as) went with his brothers, but they had planned to get rid of him. They grabbed him and threw him into a well! Then they took his shirt, put some sheep blood on it and told their father that a wolf actually **had** eaten their brother, while they were busy racing. Poor Yaqub (as) was ever so sad that his lovely son was gone. He didn't believe the brothers, and he knew that his son must be alive. He prayed to Allah for comfort.

In the weLL, ALLah made Yusuf (as) feeL better and gave him some hope.

Some men with camels and horses were travelling to Egypt. On the way, they stopped at the well that Yusuf (as) was in, to get some water. Of course they didn't know there was a young man in the well, so they were very surprised to find Yusuf (as). They wanted to sell him as a slave, which is a person who does all the hard work for someone else, with no pay. They locked him up and TOOK HIM WITH THEM.

In Egypt, a very important man bought Yusuf (as), took off his chains and kept him well.

Yusuf (as) was amazed

that a while ago he was in a well

and he didn't even know if he would stay alive,

and now he was in a palace with comfort and food!

He was grateful to ALLah.

His master saw that Yusuf (as) was honest, with good manners and charm, and someone who always did what he was told. That's why he made him in charge of his house. People all over the town heard of Yusuf, who was

the most handsome man anyone had ever seen.

BUT THINGS DIDN'T STAY GOOD, BECAUSE THE LADY OF THE HOUSE BECAME ABSOLUTELY CRAZY ABOUT YUSUF (AS) AND SHE TRIED TO MAKE HIM DO SOMETHING WHICH IS NOT ALLOWED.

When other women heard about this, they made fun of the lady of the house. So she invited them to her house and while they were cutting fruits, she asked Yusuf (as) to walk in. The ladies couldn't believe how beautiful he was! They forgot they were cutting fruit, and cut their hands instead. Then they said that he must be an angel instead of a human!

The lady still wanted him to do something that was not allowed, but Yusuf (as) said he definitely wouldn't ever do anything that Allah doesn't like. So she had him thrown into prison.

In prison, Yusuf (as) was given a gift from Allah. He could tell people what their dreams mean, which is handy, because some dreams can come true. One of the king's servants was in prison too, and Yusuf (as) told him that his dream means that he will work for the king again.

HE TOLD THE KING'S SERVANT TO LET THE KING KNOW THAT A MAN WHO HASN'T DONE ANYTHING WRONG IS IN PRISON. HE HOPED THE KING WOULD HELP.

But the king's servant FORGOT for a few years! What a forgetful head he was! Then one day, the king had a **strange** dream. He dreamt that seven skinny cows were eating seven fat cows, and other *funny* things. Nobody knew what it meant. But then the servant remembered Yusuf (as) and the king sent him to go and ask about the dream. Yusuf said that the dream was all about how much food the people would be able to grow over the years.

The king was so happy that he took Yusuf (as) out of prison,

and found proof that he had done nothing wrong. What's more, the king gave Yusuf (as) a very, very **important** job. Then came a time when people could not grow food because the earth was too *dry*. But Yusuf (as) had saved a huge amount of food from when the land was not dry. He told the king that they should sell that food to people from other places who needed it.

AND GUESS WHO TURNED UP TO BUY SOME?! YES! IT WAS YUSUF'S (AS) BROTHERS, WHO HAD THROWN HIM INTO THE WELL!

All of the brothers had come, except Binyamin (as). They didn't recognise Yusuf (as) but he sure did recognise them. He didn't tell them who he was, and he asked them to come back with Binyamin (as). Then he *secretly* put the money they had paid, back into their food bags.

When the brothers got back, they asked their father to let them take Binyamin (as) to Egypt. When they saw that the money had been given back, they *comforted* their father that the important man in Egypt wouldn't harm them. He had even returned their money!

So their father Let them take him.

When Yusuf (as) saw his brother, he told him *secretly.* that he was his long lost brother Yusuf (as).

They were both so happy that they hugged and cried!

Then Yusuf made it look as if Binyamin stole the king's golden cup.

HE DID THAT SO THAT HE COULD PRETEND HE'S PUNISHING HIM AND KEEP HIM WITH HIM.

When the brothers went back without Binyamin, their father was very, very sad. So sad that his *eyes stopped working*. He prayed to Allah and he asked his sons to please go and find both Yusuf and Binyamin.

The brothers went back to Egypt and BEGGED the important man, the Chief Minister, who they didn't know was their brother Yusuf (as), for more food, even though they didn't have much money. Yusuf (as) then told them who he was!

THEY WERE AMAZED AND SCARED,

BUT YUSUF (AS) FORGAVE THEM

AND THEY ALL HUGGED.

Then he asked them to bring his whole family to him, and he asked them to take his shirt to their father and put it over his head, because it will make his eyes all better. He was right, it made Yaqub's (as) eyes better and made him so happy that his sons were safe and alive.

When the whole family got to Egypt, they all bowed down to Yusuf (as). It was just what his dream in the beginning had shown him, with eleven stars, the sun and the moon bowing down to him. After that, they all lived happily in Egypt together.

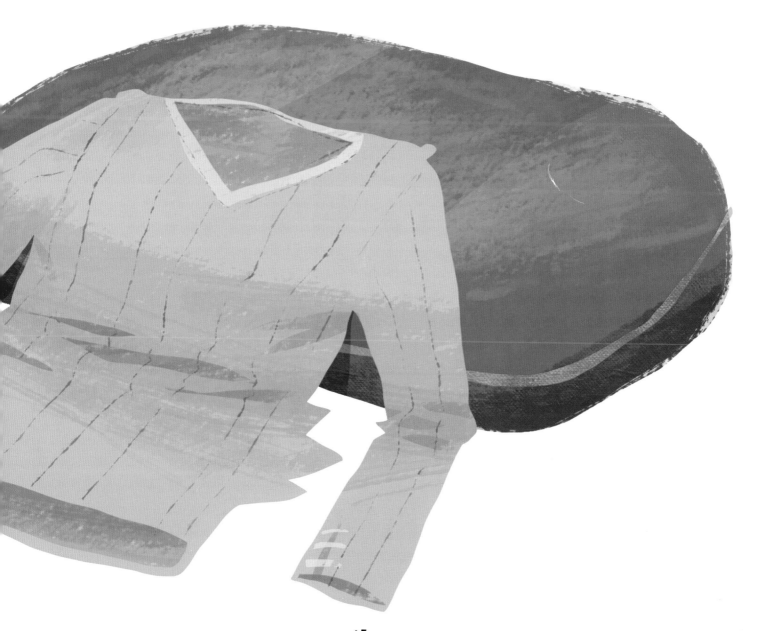

Question Time

Ali: Why were Yusuf's (as) brothers so mean to him?

Migo: Because they were jealous. Jealousy is very bad. It can make people do horrid things.

Ali: It's so lucky somebody found him in the well.

Migo: That was all part of Allah's plan.

Ali: Even going to prison?

Migo: Yes, even going to prison. If he didn't go to prison, he wouldn't have told that man what his dream means, and the man wouldn't have told the king about Yusuf (as). Even if something seems bad to us at the time, we have to remember, it's all part of Allah's plan for something good for us.

Ali: Ok Migo, I'll remember. Even when I fall off my bike!

Migo: Good lad!

AYUB

(Job)

ALAYHI SALAM

(as) was a very humble and patient man.

One day, some angels were talking about the humans, and one of them said that

on that day, Ayub (as) is the best creature on Earth,

because of how **patient** he is and how he always **remembers Allah**. He is never **proud** or **selfish** and always **gives** to the poor.

Iblis heard all this and was annoyed, because he wants humans to do **bad** things, not so many good things! So off he went to distract him from his prayers. But Ayub (as) wasn't tempted by the evil thoughts. This annoyed Iblis even more!

So Iblis went to Allah and said that Ayub (as) was only remembering Him because he had a lot of money and didn't want Him to take it away. Allah wanted to prove to Iblis that Ayub only worshipped him because of his true heart, so he let him do whatever he wanted to with Ayub's money. Iblis and his helpers took away all the money that Ayub (as) had.

But he still remembered Allah and worshipped him just the same.

Iblis was furious. He went to Allah and said that if all of Ayub's children were taken away, then he wouldn't pray to Allah anymore. So Allah let Iblis do what he wanted with Ayub's (as) children, because he knew it wouldn't make a difference. Iblis and his helpers took away all of Ayub's children.

But he still remembered Allah and worshipped him just the same.

Then Iblis and his helpers thought that taking away Ayub's (as) health would make him leave Allah, so they made him very, very sick.

But he still remembered Allah and worshipped him just the same.

One day, Ayub (as) made dua to Allah for his mercy. So Allah asked him to hit the floor with his foot and water came from there for him to wash in and drink, which

made him all better.

Then Allah gave back all his children and money. Allah had been very pleased with his patience and wanted to remind us what happens when we don't stop worshipping him.

Question Time

Migo: Let's see if you remember. Why did the angels say that Ayub is the best creature on earth?

Ali: Because he was always patient, and always, always gave money to poor people, and was never selfish.

Migo: Exactly! And he remembered Allah all the time.

Ali: And even when all his things went away, he still carried on being good and praying and everything.

Migo: Ma sha Allah, yes. That's why Allah was so happy with him and gave him all those blessings back.

Ali: He gave him special water!

Migo: I hope I can be patient if I lose things.

Ali: I'm going to hide your phone when you sleep, to test you!

Migo: Cheeky! I'm going tickle you till you say sorry!

YUNUS

(Jonah)

ALAYHI SALAM

The prophet Yunus (as) was sent to shameless people who didn't believe in Allah. He tried to tell them about Allah, but they wouldn't listen at all, so Yunus (as) got upset and went away.

AFTER HE HAD LEFT, THE SKIES WENT RED AND STARTED TO LOOK LIKE THEY WERE ON FIRE!

The people got scared, and thought that Allah must be real and he must be angry with them. So they all went to the mountain and prayed to Allah not to be angry.

It was magnificent! Allah was happy with them.

He made the sky normal again and gave them blessings.

Now the people wished Yunus (as) hadn't gone away. They wanted him to come back so he could teach them more about **Allah.**

76

Yunus (as) couldn't come back just yet, because he was on a ship.

It was a DARK night and there was a BIG

BAD STORM.

The people on the ship had to throw off all their things to make the ship lighter, but it wasn't enough. They decided that they had to throw off one man, too. They didn't want it to be Yunus (as), but his name kept coming up.

Like when you do eeny meeny miny mo.

Yunus (as) realised that it must be Allah who is making this happen. He thought that maybe Allah isn't happy with him for leaving his people. So he jumped into the sea, and just then,

HE WAS SWALLOWED BY A

HUGE, GREAT

WHALE!

Whales are as big as houses! Yunus (as) was alive in there and he started praying to Allah. He said the same dua over and over again. The words he was saying to Allah meant:

there is no one who should be worshipped except you.

There is absolutely not a thing wrong with you. I am the one who has done wrong.

All *creatures* in the sea heard this and came near the whale and said the same words!

The whale was a bit scared, because it realised it had swallowed a prophet. But it felt ok, because Allah had told it to do that.

Allah heard the *lovely* words of Yunus (as) and knew that he felt sorry. So He told the whale to take him out onto a nice, *warm* Island. The sun on the island hurt Yunus (as) because he wasn't well. So Allah gave him **shade** and forgave him.

ALLah toLd Yunus (as)

that he forgave him just because

he had prayed to him so much.

YUNUS (AS) GOT BETTER AND WENT BACK
TO HIS PEOPLE. HE WAS SO HAPPY TO
SEE THAT THEY ALL BELIEVED IN ALLAH
NOW!

THEY ALL PRAYED TOGETHER TO THANK
ALLAH AND LIVED HAPPILY.

Question Time

Migo: What did the people do to make Allah happy with them again?

Ali: They all went to the mountain and prayed and said sorry to Allah.

Migo: That's right, my fruit trifle.

Ali: Migo, do you think the whale wanted to eat him up?

Migo: No, my dear. Remember, the whale was upset because he realised he had swallowed a very special person. A prophet! Allah let the whale know what to do. And he didn't tell him to gobble him up for sure!

Ali: Was Yunus (as) scared in the whale's belly?

Migo: I don't think he was scared. He was just sorry that he had left his people and he was making a special dua, the one mentioned in the story. We still make that dua today.

MUSA

(Moses)

ALAYHI SALAM

The ruler of Egypt is called the pharaoh. The pharaoh of that time was a HORRID man who was very mean to the Children of Israel - people that are from the family of Yaqub (as).

One day, the pharaoh had a dream which meant that a boy from the Children of Israel will take over Egypt. He absolutely didn't want this, so he **ordered** that all boys born to the Children of Israel should be killed.

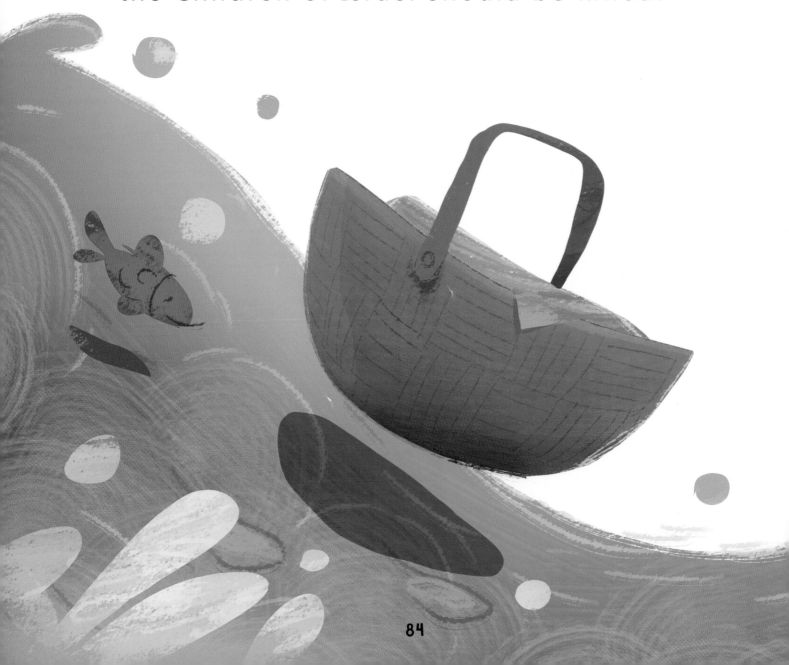

Musa's (as) mother had a baby boy called **Harun** (as), when the boys were allowed to live. But she had baby **Musa** (as) in a year that all boys had to be killed. She was sad and held him close.

Then **ALLah** let her know that she shouldn't be sad and scared because this baby will, one day, become one of his prophets. He told her to make a basket, put baby Musa (as) in it and put it in the river. So she trusted in **ALLah** and made a basket and sent Musa off in the river.

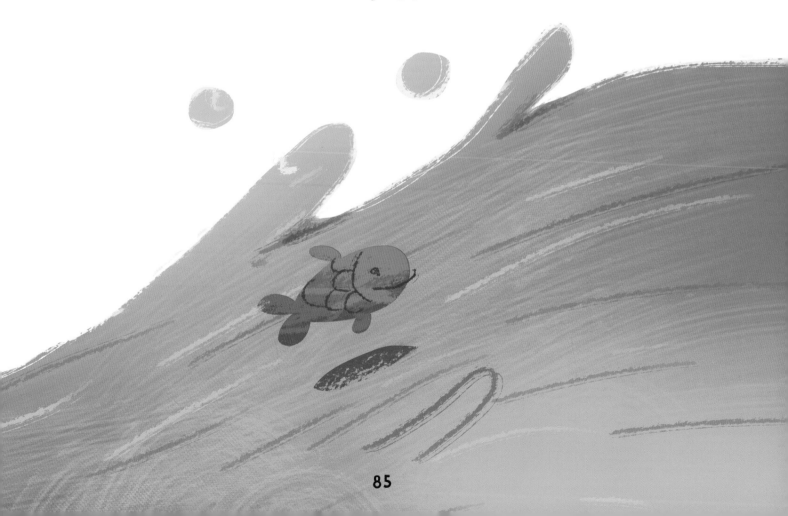

The basket went all the way down the river and stopped at the palace.

The servants found it and took it to the queen, who was pharoah's wife. The queen was not like the pharaoh. She was a good woman and she didn't have any children of her own. Allah made her love the baby when she saw him. SHE WAS SO HAPPY THAT SHE CRIED AND SHE ASKED PHARAOH TO LET HER KEEP THE BABY AS THEIR SON. Musa's mother saw him every day, because they made her their nanny to feed the baby, but nobody knew she was his mum.

Musa (as) grew up in the palace as a prince. He became strong, clever and wise. One day, two men were fighting in the city, and one was hitting the other. Musa (as) went to help, but he **accidentally** hit the man so hard that he died.

MUSA (AS) FELT VERY SAD AND HE BEGGED ALLAH TO FORGIVE HIM.

But, by Pharaoh's rules, the punishment for killing an Egyptian was to be killed. A man told Musa (as) that the chiefs were going to punish him and that he should **run away**.

Musa (as) went away quickly. He made his way to the nearest country.

When he got there he rested under a **tree.** He saw some shepherds giving their *sheep* water at a spring, so he went over. He saw two women who looked like they needed help, so he asked if he could help them. The women needed to give their *sheep* water too, but they couldn't get past the men.

Musa (as) very kindly did it for them.

Then he went to rest under the **tree** again. Soon, one of the ladies who he had helped, came over and told Musa (as) that they had told their old father how kind he had been. Their father wanted to invite him to their house to thank him. So Musa (as) went.

THE OLD MAN WAS SO HAPPY WITH MUSA (AS) THAT HE ASKED HIM IF HE WOULD LIKE TO MARRY HIS DAUGHTER AND WORK FOR HIM AS A SHEPHERD. MUSA (AS) SAID THAT HE WOULD.

MUSA (AS) WORKED AS A SHEPHERD FOR TEN YEARS.
Then one day, he decided he wanted to go back to Egypt. So he set off with his family through the desert. When they reached a mountain called Tur, it was night-time. Musa (as) noticed a fire a little far away, so he thought he would go and get a little of it on a stick, to make their own fire to keep warm.

What happened next was amazing! Allah spoke to Musa (as)! He didn't send an angel. He spoke to Musa himself!

First, He showed Musa some miracles. He asked him to *throw* down the stick that he carries with him to lean on. When he threw it down it turned into a *slithering snake*! And when he picked it up, it turned back into his stick. Then Allah asked him to put his hand in his underarm, and when he took it out it was white and shining!

90

Next, Allah asked Musa (as) to go to Pharaoh to tell him about Allah, because he is EVIL and is doing wrong things. Musa (as) said that he was a bit scared that Pharaoh would punish him if he went back, for killing the man. But Allah told him that He is with him and he would be safe. Musa (as) asked if his brother Harun (as) could also come with him and be a prophet too. Allah almighty said he could.

The brothers, Musa (as) and Harun (as), told Pharaoh about Allah and asked him to let the Children of Israel go with them - to set them *free*. The EVIL Pharaoh was as cross as ever! He said that the Children of Israel were his slaves and he would never let them go.

What's more, he said that he himself was God! And if they wanted to choose a god that wasn't him, he would throw them in **prison**! Musa (as) realised that talking to Pharaoh was no good at all, so he showed him his *miracles*. He threw down his stick and it became a *snake* and he showed his hand, which was white and shining.

Now Pharaoh was amazed, and he was scared. But he tried to say that what Musa (as) had shown was nothing but a magic trick. He called the best magicians in the country, to have a competition against Musa (as).

Little did he know,
   that what Musa (as)
      showed was from Allah,

and nothing can beat Allah!

When the magicians came they all threw down sticks that turned into *snakes*. Then Musa (as) threw his stick down and it became a **huge, giant, sLithering** *snake*, and it ate up all the other *snakes*! Then Musa picked it up and it became a stick again.

The *magicians* were amazed and believed in Allah straight away. **FURIOUS** Pharaoh said he would kill them, but they still said they believe in Allah. Pharaoh began to have important meetings to make sure the people keep thinking he is God.

He also ordered a tower to be made, which would be high enough to reach heaven, so he can see if there is a god there.

The Egyptian people were scared of Pharaoh and all started believing that Musa (as) had won the competition by tricking everyone. Pharaoh also ordered his men to start hurting the Children of Israel **really** badly.

All they could do was be patient. Musa (as) asked Pharaoh again to let the Children of Israel go. But he didn't. He called everyone and told them that he is God, because he has gold and jewels that he can help them with and Musa has nothing, he is just a poor man. the Children of Israel obeyed Pharaoh. Then Allah showed the Egyptian people some signs of punishment. He sent:

A FLOOD,

LOCUSTS,

LICE,

BLOOD IN THE river,

AND even frogs!

There were frogs everywhere! In the food, in the houses, just everywhere you looked. Each time the people promised that they would let the Children of Israel go, but then they broke their promise when

Musa (as) prayed for the punishment to end.

Many years passed and Pharaoh still wouldn't believe in Allah and wouldn't stop being cruel to the Children of Israel. Musa (as) made a dua, then Allah told him to take his people out of Egypt. They put their trust in Allah and left. They travelled at night and got to the Red Sea in the morning.

Now Pharaoh had found out that they had left and was bringing his **huge** army to get them! The Children of Israel were **scared**. In front of them was a sea and behind them was Pharaoh's army. They had nowhere to run!

Then ALLah asked Musa (as) to hit the sea with his stick. He did it, and the sea made a big gap in the middLe! The water stood on each side with a nice path in the **middle,** to walk in. They all went across. Pharaoh's army quickly came and started walking on the path in the sea, but Allah made the water go back to normal so Pharaoh and his men all drowned.

Now the Children of Israel were safe. Allah had told Musa (as) to go to the Blessed Land, Palestine. But his people were not **BRAVE** enough. They said they would not go unless nobody else lived there, in case they had to fight. Musa (as) asked Allah what to do and how to **lead** his people. Now they were in the same place where Allah had spoken to him. Allah asked him to fast for **THIRTY** days then come to the **mountain**, then he would tell him. So he did as he was asked. He fasted and then left Harun (as) in charge of the people before he went to the mountain.

When Musa (as) went to speak to Allah, he ate something just to make sure his breath didn't smell bad. But Allah told him that he *loves* the smell of a fasting person more than a rose. Allah asked him to fast for ten more days.

Musa (as) asked to see Allah with his eyes. Allah said that he couldn't let him see him, and if he looks at the mountain he will know why. ALLAH SHOWED A TEENY BIT OF HIMSELF TO THE MOUNTAIN AND IT COLLAPSED INTO DUST, BECAUSE IT COULDN'T TAKE ALLAH'S GREATNESS. Musa (as) fainted! When he woke up he said Allah is *glorious*, and asked forgiveness and said he is a believer. Then Allah gave him instructions for his people - how they should live their lives. It was called the TORAH.

Meanwhile, as Musa (as) had been gone for forty days, the people started being *silly*. One man made a golden calf out of jewellery they stole and said that it is God, and some of them actually **believed** in it! Harun (as) tried to talk sense into them, but they said they will only stop praying to the golden calf if Musa (as) comes back.

Musa (as) came back very upset and angry. He had to punish the people who chose the calf to be their God. Then he took seventy people with him and spoke to Allah again. The people should have been amazed to hear Allah's voice, but they just said that they will only believe it if they see Allah with their eyes. So Allah sent lightning and shook the ground. The people died, **but Musa (as) prayed for them, so Allah gave them Life again.**

Musa (as) suffered, for many years, patiently guiding his people who did silly things. But he was always patient and strong in his faith in Allah.

When he died,

he was peaceful,

and faithful,

and looked forward to

meeting Allah.

Question Time

Ali: So did Musa (as) grow up in the pharoah's palace?

Migo: Yes, thanks to the pharoah's wife, the queen.

Ali: How did Musa (as) beat the magicians? How did he make his snake bigger than all the other snakes?

Migo: He won because his stick turning into a snake was not a magic trick. It was a real miracle from Allah. Just like when the sea parted to allow him and his followers to pass through.

Ali: I can't believe the people made a golden baby cow and thought it could be God. That's so silly.

Migo: I'm very glad you think so, my peanut butter doughnut!

Ali: And that yucky bit about the frogs and locusts! Why did Musa (as) pray for the punishment to go away?

Migo: Because he loved his people and wanted what was best for them.

Ali: He was really nice. I wonder why the mountain became dust when it saw Allah?

Migo: It became dust because it couldn't stand the greatness of Allah. His extreme awesomeness is unbearable to see.

Ali: Does that mean we will never meet Allah?

Migo: No, we just can't see him in this life. When we go to Jannah In sha Allah we will!

DAWUD

(David)

ALAYHI SALAM

The Children of Israel were given a king chosen by **ALLah**, called Talut. He had prepared his army to fight against the enemy, whose leader was a **HUGE**, giant-like mighty warrior. His name was Galut (Goliath). To start the fight, Goliath wanted one man to fight against him. Nobody dared to do it - they were *terrified* of Goliath. The king wondered if there was anybody brave enough.

Then someone came forward to do it. He was very young and didn't look strong, but he relied on **ALLah**.

The king said that he probably wasn't strong enough,

but the young person said that he had killed a **lion** and a **bear** before, all by himself. Then he went to fight Goliath and he shot a stone at him with his sling, straight to his head. Goliath fell to the ground - dead.

The young hero was Dawud (as).

He was brave, wise, sincere and dedicated. He became an important man in the kingdom. Even though he was a **HERO**, Dawud (as), was humble.

He went into the desert just to think about **ALLah** and glorify Him. His voice was so *beautiful* that even the mountains, birds and plants joined in with him to glorify **ALLah** - this was a miracle from **ALLah**. He was a **prophet,** and was given the Pslams, which is a holy book like the Quran. The other special miracle that **ALLah** gave Dawud (as) was that he could understand the languages of birds and animals!

The people absolutely **loved** Dawud (as). King Talut started to become jealous and wanted to kill him. So Dawud (as) went to hide in a cave, and after a while some people came to stay with him and be on his side. King Talut decided to go to war against Dawud (as).

Dawud (as) went to meet the king's army and found that they were resting. He tore off a piece of the sleeping king's clothes.

Then he woke him up and said,

"You were coming to get me, but I don't hate you.

I don't want to kill you.

I could've killed you now, but I didn't.

LOOK!

I cut a bit of your clothes,

BUT really, I could have harmed you,

don't you see?

I only Love!"

After some years, someone killed Talut in a battle. Dawud (as) became **KING.** So he was now a prophet and a king.

His kingdom was **strong** and great and his enemies were scared of him. He had a son called **Sulaiman/Solomon (as)**. When he died, his son called the birds to protect Dawud and the people at the funeral from the hot sun.

ALLah's prophet Dawud (as) was buried.

Question Time

ALi: Migo! This story means that even if you're short or small, you can do really cool things. Even things that other big people can't do.

Migo: Exactly! You just have to trust in ALLah, and be smart.

ALi: I can't believe the mountains and birds and plants joined Dawud (as) when he was saying how great ALLah is! I want to hear his voice!

Migo: Me too, ALi.

ALi: But why didn't he just kiLL that horrible king? Why did he only cut up his clothes?

Migo: Because, my little cinnamon bun, Dawud (as) was extremely smart, and kind and Loving. He didn't want to hurt anybody, and he knew that if he uses Love instead of violence, then the king would be his friend.

ALi: And then he became King!

Migo: Yes he did!

SULAIMAN

(Solomon)

ALAYHI SALAM

Sulaiman (as) was Dawud's (as) son. He was a prophet and he became King after his father died. Sulaiman (as) was blessed by Allah, by being able to do many things that humans cannot do. He could tell the **winds** which way to blow. He could understand and talk to animals and birds in **their** language. And Allah taught him how to use metals, deep inside the earth, to make tools and weapons. Sulaiman's (as) army didn't only have men, it had **birds** and animals, like **Lions** too! It also had **jinns**, which are another one of Allah's creatures that are good or evil, just like humans.

One day, Sulaiman's army was **marching** through a valley. An ant saw them coming and quickly went to tell the other ants to get out of the way, otherwise Sulaiman and his army might crush them under their feet, by accident. Sulaiman (as) heard the ant,

and he smiled because he was happy that the ant knew that he would never harm them, or any creature, on purpose.

He thanked ALLah for saving their Lives.

Sulaiman (as) built a **huge** temple for people to worship Allah. From there, Sulaiman (as) and his people went for *Hajj.* to Makkah.

One day, Sulaiman (as) was looking for the **hoopoe** bird. When the bird finally came to him, he said that he was late because he had come from a place called Sheba, where the Queen and her people had everything they needed, but prayed to the SUN instead of Allah!

So Sulaiman sent a **letter** to the Queen, with the bird. The **letter** said that they should believe in Allah. The Queen was not sure what to do, so she sent a gift from her treasure to Sulaiman. She thought that this way, she could see how big Sulaiman's army is. When her messengers took the gift, they saw his INCREDIBLE army, with **amazing** things and soldiers which were fearsome **Lions** and **tigers**! What's more, they saw how rich the palace was! It was made from gold and sandalwood.

Sulaiman (as) told them that he did not need their gift, but he only wanted them to believe in Allah. They went back and told their queen about all the wonderful things they had seen and told her what Sulaiman (as) had said.

The queen decided she would go to visit Sulaiman (as) herself. But before she got there, Sulaiman had asked a jinn to bring her throne to his palace. The jinn brought the throne all the way from another country in less than a second! This is a miracle. When the queen saw her throne, and saw the amazing palace, she couldn't believe her eyes! The floor was made of glass and it was shimmering. She lifted her dress up, to walk, because she thought it was water.

SHE REALISED THAT SULAIMAN (AS) MUST BE A MESSENGER OF ALLAH. SHE REALISED THE SUN IS ONLY A THING MADE BY ALLAH, AND SHE AND HER PEOPLE STOPPED PRAYING TO THE SUN.

SULAIMAN (AS) ALWAYS TRIED TO TEACH HIS PEOPLE (AND JINN), THAT NO CREATURE KNOWS EVERYTHING, ONLY ALLAH KNOWS EVERYTHING. EVEN THE WAY SULAIMAN (AS) DIED TAUGHT THE PEOPLE THIS. HE WAS WATCHING OVER THE JINN WHEN THEY WERE WORKING, SO THEY CARRIED ON WORKING HARD BECAUSE HE WAS THERE. THEN HE DIED, QUIETLY, SITTING DOWN AND STAYED LIKE THAT. FOR DAYS HE SAT THERE AND NOBODY KNEW HE WAS DEAD, SO THE JINNS KEPT WORKING. THEN AN ANT ATE THE STICK HE WAS LEANING ON AND HIS GREAT BODY FELL. THIS PROVES THAT THE JINN DO NOT KNOW EVERYTHING, OTHERWISE THEY WOULD HAVE KNOWN THAT THE PROPHET SULAIMAN (AS) DIED. THE PROPHET'S LIFE AND DEATH WERE WONDROUS!

Question Time

Migo: Ok Ali, if you can tell me the things that Sulaiman (as) could do that other humans can't do, you'll get a big bear hug.

Ali: He was like a superhero with powers. He could control the winds, talk to animals and make things out of metal!

Migo: Fantastic. He was a real superhero. Not like those pretend ones you have in your cartoons.

Ali: Cool!

Migo: It said that he had jinns in his army, but do you know what they are?

Ali: Scary monsters!

Migo: Haha. They can be good and they can be bad, just like humans. They are another creature that Allah made, but we can't see them.

Ali: Can they see us?

Migo: Yes.

Ali: I wonder if there are still people who can talk to animals like Sulaiman alayhi salaam did?

Migo: Haha! No, my boy, there aren't. Only in their imagination. Allah gave that special power to his prophet, only, and there are no more prophets now. Muhammad (saw) was the last one. But everyone should be very kind to animals and understand what they want and need.

ZAKARIYAH

(Zechariah)

&

YAHYA

(John)

ALAYHIMA SALAM

The prophet Zakariyah (as) was the one who was in charge of looking after Mariam (as) - we will hear that story later. He was an old man and he didn't have any children yet. He worried about that. He worried that if he didn't have any children,

nobody would keep reminding the people about Allah, after he passed away.

So he thought he would ask Allah for a child, because whenever he asked Allah for something, he always got it!

Then one day, the angels said to Zakariyah (as) that he will be having a little baby boy called Yahya/John.

"Really?! But how can I when I am an old man and my wife can't have children?" said Zakariyah.

Allah said that's not a problem for Him,

He can make anything happen, anything at all.

Allah told him to not speak for three days and remember his lord morning and evening.

Yahya (as) was a very **special** child. While all the other children were cruel to animals, he was lovely to them. He gave them his food, and ate fruit from trees instead. He loved to read when he was a little boy, and so he became the **wisest** man around, who knew lots more than others. When he grew up, he was even more kind to his **parents** and to all creatures.

He always thought about ALLah.

He loved to be out in the open and food wasn't important to him. Sometimes, he would go to a cave to sit and there would be a **Lion** or a **bear**,

and the animal would just bow its head and walk away, because it knew that this man is Yahya (as), the prophet who cares for animals.

When Yahya (as) talked to people about Allah, they cried with love for Allah. Some other people did not like that. They didn't want people to know about Allah and to worship Him. Those people had Yahya (as) killed in a very horrible way. They did not realise how angry that would make Allah. They were punished with armies, who came to invade their lands.

Question Time

Migo: Allah gave prophet Zakariyah (as) a baby when he thought it would be impossible! What does that tell you, Ali?

Ali: That if you ask Allah for something, he can do it.

Migo: Yes! You just have to really believe that Allah will do it for you. And you have to be super good!

Ali: I will!

Migo: And what was special about Yahya (as)?

Ali: He was so, so, so kind to animals and his parents and everyone! Even lions knew who he was!

Migo: Yes! And he loved reading books and talking about Allah to people.

Ali: I love books too.

Migo: Ma sha Allah, my gingernut cookie.

Ali: Haha! Your tummy is rumbling again.

ESA
(Jesus)
ALAYHI SALAM

Everybody has heard of the prophet Jesus (as). But first, I am going to tell you about his *mother*, Mariam/Mary (as). Her parents, Imran and Hannah (as), were very **good** people. They really, really wanted a baby. Mariam's mum was so happy when she found out she's having a baby, that she promised Allah the baby would stay in the temple every day, to *pray*. And so Mariam (as) spent all of her days in the temple. Everyone got together to decide who should look after her while she's there, and the chosen person was prophet Zakariyah (as). He made her a room in the temple where nobody but him could go. One day, he went to check on her and he saw that she had all kinds of **fruits** to eat. He didn't give her the fruits and nobody else could have, so he asked where they came from. She said they were from Allah and that Allah can give anything he wants, to anyone he wants. Zakariyah (as) realised that she is very special to Allah, and he taught her and guided her.

One day, an *angel* came to Mariam (as), but he came as a human. Mariam (as) got scared. The angel told her he was there to tell her that she will have a baby son. Now, usually a lady needs a husband for a baby to be born. But Mariam (as) didn't have a husband. She said that she never had a man near her, so how can it be that she is having a baby. The angel told her

it's what ALLAh wants - for that baby to be a sign for everyone and a mercy to them - It's easy for ALLah to do that.

Mariam (as) felt a baby inside her and she started getting worried about what people would say, because she is having a baby without a husband. So she left the temple and went to Nazareth. Then some time later she left Nazareth again because she was worried. She didn't get very far. She sat down under a palm tree which was all dried up, so it didn't have fruits on it.

Then her baby was born! She was very worried about what people would say. Just then, she heard a voice telling her not to worry and to shake the tree and fresh fruit will fall from it for her and that there is also a stream of water for her.

She felt happy because this miracle meant that ALLah is with her.

But she was still a bit worried.

Then the baby Esa (as) spoke!

He told her not to worry and that he would talk to the people to tell them. When Mariam (as) went back to the city, the people started telling her off.

But then Esa (as) spoke and told them that he is a prophet and ALLah has given him the book and blessed him.

Most people were AMAZED and believed this MIRACLE.

As Esa (as) grew up there were more signs that he was a prophet. But as he became a man, he saw that the people weren't doing what Musa (as) had taught them. Over the years they had started changing things and

MAKING UP THEIR OWN RULES.

They had made up what was allowed and what was not allowed. When Zakariyah and Yahya (as) passed away,

ALLah almighty asked Esa (as) to

start talking to the people about the right way to be.

To teLL them aLL about ALLah.

He wanted the people to be kind to each other. But the priests were annoyed because they thought that Esa (as) wanted to take over and to bring a new religion.

Esa (as) was given many amazing miracles! Allah allowed him to be able to heal people, bring dead people back to life, make a bird out of clay and make it come alive, and to be able to tell people what is in their houses without even looking!

One day, Esa's (as) people asked him for a table of food to be sent down from heaven. So he asked ALLah for it. ALLah said he would send it, but after that if anyone says they do not believe in ALLah, they will be punished.

And the table of food came down

with a cloud at the top,

and a cloud at the bottom.

Thousands of people ate that food but it still didn't finish!

Esa (as) kept teaching the people about ALLah and how to Live. But the evil people decided to have him killed. Little did they know that ALLah protected his prophet!

ALLAH TOOK ESA (AS) BACK UP TO THE HEAVENS.

The evil people got hold of a man who ALLah had made to Look exactly Like Esa (as), and that man was killed by those horrid people on a cross.

Question Time

Ali: I can't believe Esa (as) spoke when he was a baby! How did that happen Migo?

Migo: Anything Allah wants can happen, sugar plum. Allah made him able to talk, because then the people would believe Mariam (as), and know that this really was a miracle of Allah.

Ali: And he had more miracles!

Migo: Yes, like healing people, making dead come back to life and making a clay bird come to life. Allah did all of that so his people become believers.

Ali: But Migo, some people say that Esa is the son of God...

Migo: Yes Ali, Christians do believe that, but we Muslims know he is not. He is a messenger of Allah. We know that Allah has no children and no parents.

Ali: Ok Migo, Can I jump on your belly now?

Migo: Only if you can catch me first you cheeky monkey.

MUHAMMAD

SAL ALLAHU ALAIHI WA SALAM

The prophet Muhammad (saw) became an orphan when he was a young child. When he was six, his mum and dad were not with him anymore and he was looked after by his GRANDFATHER and then his UNCLE, Abu Talib. He grew up taking care of his uncle's sheep.

He was such a good boy, that everybody called him 'AL-Ameen' (the faithful).

As a young man, he married Khadijah (ra), and they looked after each other very well and were very happy. He was known to be very **kind** and to help needy people.

One day, the people of Makkah were having a big old **argument** because they were making the Kaaba new and were fighting about who would put on the most important part- the **black stone**. They decided that the first person to come in through the gate would decide what to do. They were all very happy that it was Muhammad (saw),

because they aLL trusted him very much.

He had a great idea. He told them to put the stone on a cloth and everybody should hold the cloth together to bring the black stone to its place.

Everyone was happy.

Muhammad (saw) had children with his wife Khadijah (ra) and he also helped his uncle look after his little cousin Ali (ra).

The Prophet was so *lovely* and *kind* that one day a little boy, called Zaid (ra), who worked in the house for the family, refused to go home with his **own father** - even though the Prophet said he could if he wanted to. He said he wanted to stay with Muhammad (saw). When the Prophet heard

this, he told everybody that he is *adopting* Zaid (ra) as his own son!

Muhammad (saw) was not very happy with the way people behaved.

They prayed to statues and were not very nice to each other.

He used to go to a cave and stay there for a Long time,

just thinking about the world and beyond.

Then one day, in that cave in Mount Hira,

the **angel Jibreel** came to him.

The angel asked him to read. The Prophet said that he *couldn't* read. So the angel squeezed him and asked him to read again. But the Prophet again said that he *couldn't*. The angel again held him and asked him to

READ IN THE NAME OF THE LORD, WHO HAS CREATED HUMANS AND EVERYTHING THAT THERE IS!

THE WORDS THE ANGEL SAID AT THAT TIME ARE THE WORDS IN THE FIRST FIVE AYATS OF SURAH AL-ALAQ IN THE QURAN.

The prophet then said the words. He went back to his wife, thinking that he may be seeing things and going crazy. But Khadijah (ra) said that Allah would never allow that to happen to him because he is a **great** man. She went to see her cousin Waraqa, who knew a lot about Jews and Christians and prophets who had come before.

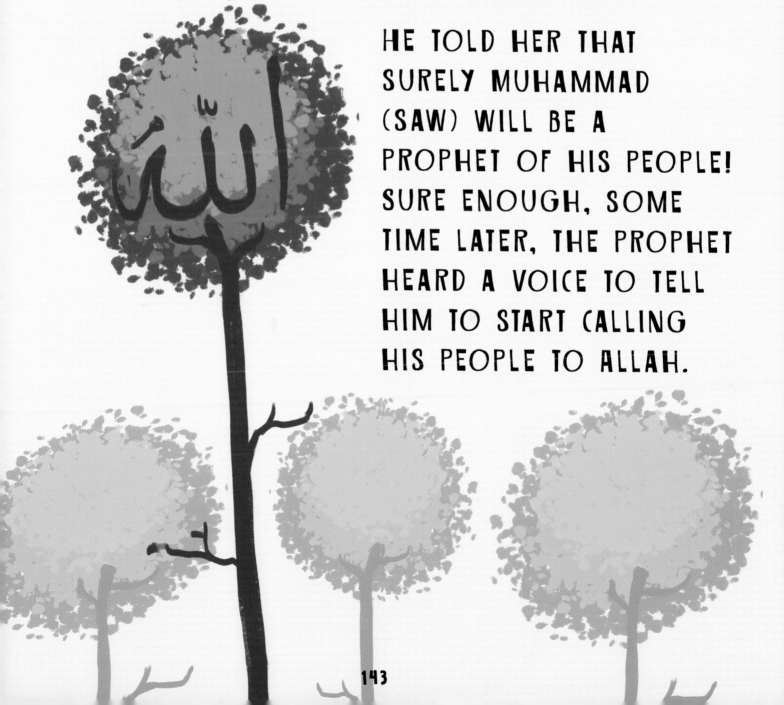

HE TOLD HER THAT SURELY MUHAMMAD (SAW) WILL BE A PROPHET OF HIS PEOPLE! SURE ENOUGH, SOME TIME LATER, THE PROPHET HEARD A VOICE TO TELL HIM TO START CALLING HIS PEOPLE TO ALLAH.

The first person to believe was Khadijah (ra), his wife. The next was Ali and then Zaid (ra). Abu Bakr (ra) was an **important** man in Makkah at that time and he was one of the people who became a Muslim. For many years, the Prophet *patiently* taught people about Allah. At first, secretly, and then to everyone out loud. Many people became Muslim, even the Prophet's uncle Hamza (ra), who was as brave as a LION!

But as usual, as you know now, when a prophet brings the message of Allah, there are people who aren't terribly happy. The same thing happened at the Prophet's time. Those people that weren't happy were worried about their PRIDE and their money, that's all. They were the **controllers** of Makkah - the *Quraish*. They did some very cruel things to the Prophet. But he was patient, as usual, and didn't do anything back.

When the *Quraish* saw that more and more people were becoming Muslims, they really got in a huff. They decided to start torturing the poor believers. But guess what? The believers stayed **strong** and would not stop.

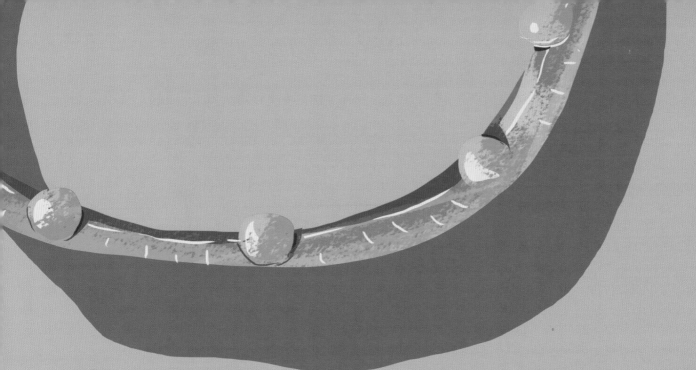

The people even tried to stop the Prophet

from teaching about Islam,

by saying that they would give
him more money

than anyone has,

and make him
their king.

But of
course, our
dear Prophet
didn't want
the riches.

The Quraish were being even more cruel and making the Muslims' lives very hard, so the Prophet said that some of them should go to Abyssinia, because there is a pious king there who is a good man.

THAT KING WAS A CHRISTIAN AND HE WAS VERY KIND TO THE PEOPLE WHO WENT TO HIS COUNTRY TO BE SAFE.

EVEN WHEN MEN FROM THE QURAISH CAME TO TAKE THEM AWAY, HE LISTENED TO THE MUSLIMS' SIDE OF THE STORY ABOUT ISLAM AND DIDN'T LET ANYONE HARM THEM.

Meanwhile, back in Makkah the Prophet kept on bringing people to Islam. More and more people were becoming Muslim. The Quraish were furious and tried to get his uncle to stop him, but his uncle protected him, even though he didn't become a Muslim. At this time Umar (ra) also became a Muslim.

THEN FOR THREE WHOLE YEARS, THE PROPHET AND HIS FOLLOWERS, WERE MADE TO LIVE CUT OFF FROM THE PEOPLE WHO DIDN'T BELIEVE. IT WAS VERY HARD FOR THEM TO GET FOOD.

148

Then came a very sad year for the Prophet. His uncle, Abu Talib, and his wife Khadijah both passed away. His uncle was the one who had been like his father and had been so kind to him and protected him. He was going to miss his wonderful wife who he loved very much.

One day, the Prophet was telling a group of people about Allah. Some of them were from a city called Yathrib (then later it was called Madina). They became believers and went and told their people about the Prophet. Now, when it had been twelve years since the prophet started calling people to Allah,

a very special thing happened.

The Prophet went on a journey from Makkah to Jerusalem and then to heaven!

Yes, it's amazing! This is called the Miraj. First his heart was washed and he went on the Buraq, which is sort of like a horse, but it can go very far very quickly.

During this journey, the Prophet met and said salaam to the other prophets in heaven. Also, here, Allah told the Prophet that his people have to pray **Salah** five times a day. At first, Allah actually said fifty times, but then made it less for us when the Prophet asked him to, because Musa (as) told him we would find it too **hard**.

After that, some people came from Yathrib (Madina) to make a **promise** to the Prophet to be good Muslims and to be good to him. Some time later,

THE PROPHET ACTUALLY WENT TO LIVE IN MADINA.

That moving from his home in Makkah to Madina is called the *Hijrah*. When the Prophet and his friends lived there, the city became Madina. The mosque of the Prophet is built in a place that the Prophet's *camel* chose, by kneeling down there.

The people of Madina were called the Ansar, the Helpers of the Prophet.

The Prophet and all the people lived there *happily*. Some rules were made, which included that the Jews would also live there just as *happily* as the Muslims.

But guess what, those NAUGHTY people in Makkah did not give up! They still wanted to harm the Prophet and the Muslims. They marched 1000 men to Madina, to attack. The Muslims got together 300 men to fight back and **protect** themselves. Even though there were many more men on the other side, they lost the battle and the Muslims won. This is called the **Battle of Badr.**

Later there was another battle between the Quraish and the Muslims, called the **Battle of Uhud.** This time, the people from Makkah really wanted to make sure they win. They got 3000 men, 200 horses and lots of great WEAPONS. The Prophet (saw) had a lot less men and only one horse. They lost this battle, sadly, because some of his men didn't LISTEN to the Prophet's orders. Even Hamza (ra) was killed. The Quraish behaved very badly and rudely at that time.

Another time, they marched ten thousand men to Madina, to attack. But the Muslims dug a deep **moat** around Madina and **protected** it with the small number of men they had.

The Quraish men couldn't get in, though they sure did try. They started running out of food and at last, when a *STORM* came and blew away their tents, they all ran off back home.

Six years after the Prophet and his people had moved to Madina, they wanted to go to see the **Kaabah** and pray. But when they got near, the Quraish stopped them. Then they all decided to make some **rules** to have peace between everybody. The Quraish said that the Muslims could come back next year for Hajj and stay for three days and have Makkah to themselves - and that's exactly what they did.

The Prophet sent the message of Islam to far away places,
WHERE KINGS WERE RULERS.

He sent messengers with letters.
Some leaders listened nicely
AND OTHERS DID NOT.

After almost eight years since the *Hijrah*, the Quraish broke the rules of peace, by attacking friends of the Muslims. So the Prophet thought it was time to **stop** these people in Makkah from doing wrong things. He marched *ten thousand* men to Makkah. The man called Abu Sufyan, who was sent to speak to them, became a Muslim, when the Prophet spoke to him. The Prophet and the Muslims entered Makkah, and not many people tried to stop them.

They came peacefully.

Makkah was now a city of the Muslims.
The Prophet ordered all the statues, that used to be worshiped, to be broken.

Then he spoke to all the **people**. Many, many more people became Muslim.

While in Makkah, the Prophet kept spreading the message of Islam *peacefully.*.

When one of his men didn't do it peacefully, without hurting anyone, the Prophet was very sad and sent lots of money to the widows and orphans. Then he went back to Madina and kept spreading the message. Slowly all the people around became Muslims and there was no more praying to STATUES. Everyone was living nicely, with brotherhood and love.

When the Prophet felt that he might not live much longer, he went for Hajj with thousands and thousands of Muslims. He stood on the top of Mount Arafat and spoke to the people. In that speech, he reminded everyone that they will meet Allah one day. He told them to be good to their wives and their husbands. He told them that if they have slaves they should give them the same clothes and food as they have themselves, and never be cruel to them. Then he said to Allah that he has given the message of Islam to his people and the people all said that he sure had. Then, after doing the Hajj, he went back to Madina.

The Prophet (saw) lived in Madina for the last year of his life and became sick. He asked everyone for forgiveness and made sure he didn't owe anyone any money before he died.

HE DIED IN THE HOUSE OF HIS WIFE, AISHA (RA), RIGHT NEXT TO HER.

The people were very sad.

Some said they would not believe that he is dead. But the wise Abu Bakr (ra) reminded everyone that yes Muhammad (saw) has died, because he was just a human and Allah's messenger, but **Allah Almighty** will never die.

The Prophet was buried where he died. May the peace and blessings of **Allah** be upon him.

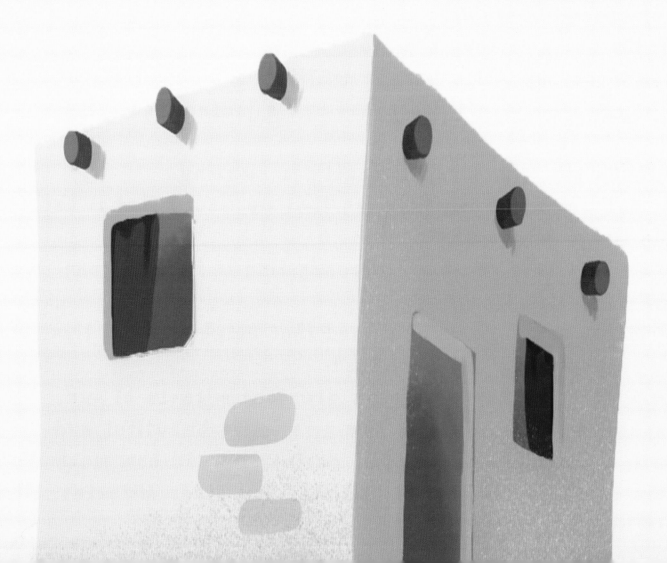

Question Time

Ali: Why couldn't the Prophet (saw) read? Didn't he go to school?

Migo: In those days, not many people could read. It wasn't something that everyone learns to do, like we do these days.

Ali: But he must have been so nice to children. That's why Zaid (ra) wanted to stay with him.

Migo: He sure was. He used to be very affectionate towards kids. Kidding around with them, and kissing them. That's how all adults should be with kids.

Ali: You're like that with me Migo! Are you copying the Prophet?

Migo: Haha. Yes! We should all copy the Prophet. He set the best examples for us.

Ali: I'm going to copy him too.

Migo: Good, my little banana truffle!

Ali: I can't believe the prophet had a journey, on a flying horse, to heaven!

Migo: Ah yes, the Miraj, It really is amazing.

Ali: But why did Musa (as) say that we would find it hard to pray fifty times a day?

Migo: Well look at us, we already find it hard to pray five times, don't we?

Ali: Haha, yes, I guess it's good that Allah made it five. Did the prophet have any miracles?

Migo: Yes. The Quran was the greatest miracle of our prophet (saw), because of how amazingly beautiful and poetic the words are, and it's perfection, and how much it tells us about Science. But he also had other miracles, like splitting the moon.

ALi: Wow! But what happened after he died? Who told people about ALLah then? Because he's the Last one and no more prophets came after him.

Migo: Yes, you're right. Prophet Muhammad (saw) is the Last and final messenger. After him, other people were in charge, the first Caliph was Abu Bakr (ra). But now we have to teLL the people about ALLah. Now it's our job. The best way we can do that is by being good MusLims and being kind, peaceful, generous and pious, Like the Prophet. By never saying bad words or harming people, and by trusting in ALLah.

ALi: Ok Migo, I promise I wiLL.

Migo: Me too, honey pie.

More fantastic titles by Muslim Children's Books Ltd

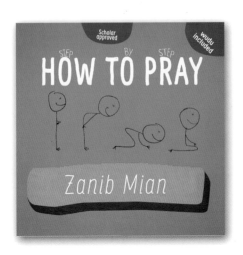

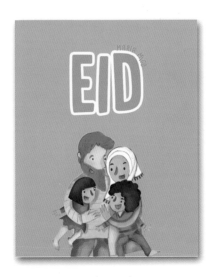

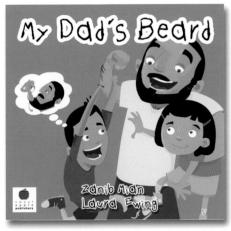

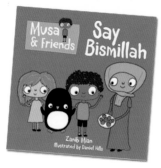

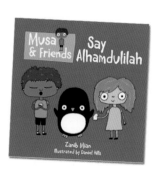

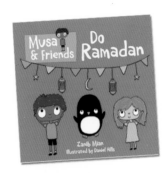

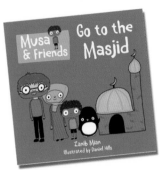

www.muslimchildrensbooks.co.uk